Social Media
secrets

The experts tell all!

About the author

Carolyn Boyes is an author, trainer and coach who works with individuals and businesses on a range of subjects including communication, strategy, personal and business brand, career management, leadership, social media and writing. She is the author of *Communication*, *Career Management* and *NLP*, also in the **business secrets** series.

Social Media
secrets

William Collins
An imprint of HarperCollins*Publishers*
1 London Bridge Street
London SE1 9GF

www.WilliamCollinsBooks.com

This Collins paperback edition published in Great Britain by William Collins in 2020

First published in Great Britain in 2020 by HarperCollins*Publishers*
Published in Canada by HarperCollins*Canada*. www.harpercollins.ca
Published in Australia by HarperCollins*Australia*. www.harpercollins.au
Published in India by *HarperCollinsPublishersIndia*. www.harpercollins.co.in

1

Copyright © HarperCollins*Publishers* 2020

Carolyn Boyes asserts the moral right to be identified as the author of this work

A catalogue record for this book
is available from the British Library

ISBN 978-0-00-838983-3

Typeset by Palimpsest Book Production Limited, Falkirk, Stirlingshire
Printed and bound by CPI Group (UK) Ltd, Croydon CR0 4YY

MIX
Paper from
responsible sources
FSC **FSC™ C007454**
www.fsc.org

This book is produced from independently certified FSC™ paper
to ensure responsible forest management.

For more information visit: www.harpercollins.co.uk/green

Contents

Learn how social media can be your best business secret

Social media is essential to businesses and anyone who already has, or wants to have, a career in business. Through social media you can talk to people, learn new information and gain new clients. You can build a business brand across international boundaries, cutting out middlemen and saving costs.

My own background in business began when talking to clients around the world meant sending letters, taking long flights or making very expensive phone calls. The advent of emails made communication easier but still limited contact to a targeted list of clients. Social media has changed everything.

When social media first came along it seemed to be just another form of entertainment. People quickly realized that it was fun to have conversations with strangers, post pictures of their cat playing the piano or comment on a newspaper blog. However, businesses soon realized that social media could be used as advertising. Now social media has progressed even further and become a vital part of any business strategy.

If I want to find a client I no longer need to identify them one by one. Once I have clients I don't need to phone or visit them. Instead, using social media, I can keep in touch with anyone anywhere in the world and show them what I have to offer using words, pictures and video. Social media is now a gigantic global conversation and a global business must.

   Business Secrets: Social Media consists of 50 **secrets** in total, divided into seven chapters.

■ **Plan.** Start afresh. Learn how the world has changed and that social media is the most effective tool for the success of your business.
■ **Promote.** The whole world can become your marketplace. Think how you can build a community of followers who will turn into customers for your business.
■ **Post.** There are so many different social media tools now. Discover which ones you should use and what the best ways are to use them.
■ **Position.** Use social media to build a long-term brand on the web which will grow your business for years to come.
■ **Monitor.** By keeping in touch with what your customers want you can consistently tweak your social media presence and make it effective.
■ **Be real.** Social media is entertaining and fun. Don't just have a business conversation: be human. Be entertaining.
■ **Follow web etiquette.** Observe some basic guidelines and legalities online just as much as you do in your offline business.

   If you follow these seven chapters, you will know everything you need to know in order to use social media effectively for yourself and your business. People will know about you and your brand and, more importantly, they will want to become your clients.

Social media isn't just fun, it's also the future of your business.

Plan

The world has changed. The mindset of the business world has had to shift enormously from even a few years ago. Over the last decade we have seen the globalization of the marketplace and an enormous appetite to buy, research and socialize online. No business can afford to be offline now. But a website is not enough. You need a strategy for multiple social media platforms.

1.1

Ditch the old thinking

In the past, if you had a business you probably had an office, possibly a shop, and you advertised your products or services in the press and via a website. You would broadcast without really knowing who was listening to you. If a customer wanted to give feedback to a business they would need to write a letter and wait for a response. Now so many people use social media the whole process has been speeded up: from weeks to seconds.

Social media and old media are very different. With old media you could only have a one-way conversation between the business and its prospective customers. You can talk to your customers and they can talk back to you. There are other differences, too:

■ Old media markets to a mass, unknown audience. Social media is a way of tailoring your marketing to one person at a time.
■ Old media is written by professional marketers. Much of social media content is generated by users and commentators in response to what you post.
■ Social media channels are open, democratic and responsive. Content can be forwarded and adapted by its users, unlike with old media.

"TV took 30 years to reach 50 million people. Facebook took 2 years" **Anon**

one minute wonder Think about marketing your business on social media in a professional way. Do your research and look at which channels your users follow. Not every channel will be used by the same type of user. Start by thinking about the top five reasons why you want or need to use social media.

■ Marketing on old media is usually highly edited and polished. Posts and commentary on social media are rougher but often more authentic.
■ Users pay to access old media: newspapers, magazines and TV. Social media is usually free for the user. You can access it when you want and from where you want.
■ Old media is controlled by the owners and the business which pays for the content. Social media content is jointly controlled by the user.
■ Old media is often focused on people in a particular country. Social media is global.

You can use social media to share news and expertise, upload product images and videos, write a weekly blog and start discussions. It can become a promotional tool for your business; helping to build your business brand and customer base as well as your profits.

Create a marketing plan that suits social media, not old media.

1.2

Know your channels

Social media sites are known as channels and social media can be accessed via the internet or apps. The number of channels is expanding all the time and its influence on our lives is growing.

If you have a business you can use social media to win customers and build a brand in a fun and entertaining way across global borders. Although new channels are added all the time, here are some you must get to know if you are going to promote your business effectively:

■ **Facebook** is one of the most popular social networks in the world. Every day it is used by billions of people. Individuals, groups and businesses all have Facebook profiles.

■ **Twitter** is a 'microblogging' site – a place where you can write short posts of up to 140 characters. It has become a source for people to get instant information on the news and post comments and pictures, even videos and links to blogs.

■ **LinkedIn** is the biggest professional social networking site. Employers increasingly expect professionals to provide a link to their LinkedIn profile before getting hired.

■ **YouTube** is the largest video broadcasting and sharing site of content such as vlogs (video blogs), music videos, talks and movie-making. Find everything from funny videos to how-to videos on here.

"These days, social media waits for no one" **Aaron Lee**

one minute wonder Take the time to look at how your competitors are using these channels to create social networks and online communities by tweeting, blogging, posting and sharing. Social media is very different from advertisement-buying activities and other types of digital marketing.

■ **Instagram** is a highly popular sharing site for photos and short videos and has helped the craze for celebrity 'selfies' – a picture of yourself.
■ **Pinterest** is a place where you can create your own pinboard of images that you have collected and share them with your followers on the web.
■ **Tumblr** is similar to Pinterest. Here, you can set up a blog, determine a theme and post all sorts of content.
■ **Snapchat** is an instant messaging mobile social network. It is based around the idea of videos and photos that self-destruct after viewing.
■ **Vine** is a video-sharing app. The short (up to six-second) videos can be embedded in a tweet or shared in emails or on other sites.

Use social media to make your products and services easily accessible and desirable.

1.3

Create a brand

What makes businesses successful is that they are always clear about their brand and where they are positioned in their marketplace.

The idea of a brand is simple. It is the thing for which you are most recognized. For example, London has Big Ben, Paris the Eiffel Tower, Nepal is known for Mount Everest. Think about a business like Virgin. Richard Branson, the owner, cleverly created a brand around himself and his business, creating a memorable name and image.

You don't need to own a multi-million-pound business to have a great brand. Some of the best brands on the web are one-person brands. Even teenagers, posting comments and producing videos from their bedrooms, are creating valuable brands on social media. A brand is an interpretation of yourself and you can show off that interpretation across Twitter, Instagram, Google Plus or any platform you choose.

case study Zoella is a hugely successful vlogger on YouTube and has created a strong brand from small beginnings. She films short videos of interest to her audience and has a big teenage following. Her brand has been so successful that it went offline. She makes

"Setting up an account is not a strategy" *Businessweek*

Think about what is at the core of your brand and how you want to show that to your social media audience.

■ What do I do for a living? Do I want my brand to be around me, the person, or around the business I am involved in?
■ What is my Mount Everest? What am I most known for? What is the core of my business?
■ What is unique about my business? What makes me stand out from my competitors or other people like me?
■ Why would people be interested in listening to what I have to tell them? When I meet people at a party, what do they ask me about?

If you don't have all the answers immediately, that's fine. It's better to take your time than rush into social media and change your brand. That will just confuse people.

Think about what you stand for and how to differentiate yourself from your competition.

appearances off screen and was even asked to write a book which sold in large numbers to her fans. Her brand was helped by the fact that she dated another successful YouTube star and they have made videos together, creating an even-better-known joint brand.

1.4

Make a promise

Most of social media is free so commitment to a brand isn't shown with money but with attention or inattention. To get that attention you need to offer a promise to people.

What difference do you want to make? What impact do you want to make? All great brands promise us something. Take a brand like Coca-Cola or Pepsi. Many drinks quench your thirst, so why buy a branded drink which costs more? Simply because the brand seems to promise more.

Some brands last for generations even though the products are very different. What do Disney, McDonald's, Twinings and Burberry really promise you that keeps you loyal to them? We will all pay more if someone or something makes us feel better. That's why advertisers show us adverts populated with people we want to aspire to be like. For some of us, that means buying a product associated with the perfect home and family; for others it means a link with being young and fashionable or being different and anti-establishment.

Sometimes the brand promise is obvious and sometimes it takes time to think through. Start by considering what makes your business stand out from its competitors. By knowing what makes you different you can work out what you are really promising to give people when they connect with your brand.

"Your brand is the single most important investment you can make in your business" Steve Forbes

Take a political information company, for example. What makes them different? Information is available from dozens of sites on the web. For one company it may be their humorous presentation of the news, for another the fact they are always first with the news or they have politicians rather than journalists working for them, so they are the first to learn about what really goes on in the corridors of power.

Perhaps you run a bakery. Isn't selling cakes and bread and buns just about feeding people? Not necessarily. Perhaps it's the way your posts of cakes in retro fifties' settings make people feel as if they are living the domestic goddess dream. You promise the lifestyle with every product you sell.

Think about what makes you different and what your brand can promise its customers.

1.5

Create a goal

Who would have imagined when Twitter or Facebook began that the most famous brands in the world would be competing for space with people posting updates from their bedrooms? But that's what has happened – social media is still sociable and fun but it has also become a serious platform on which to do business, and one-person bands can compete with the big players.

However, there's no point getting involved in social media and just setting up accounts here and there because everyone else is doing it. Take an inventory of what you are already doing and what your competitors are doing, then **SMART**:

■ **S is for Specific.** Be specific with your goals. Set some objectives for how many channels you are going to use, and what you are seeking to achieve.
■ **M is for Measurable.** All your goals should be measurable so you know whether you are achieving them or not.
■ **A is for Achievable.** What is it going to take to achieve your goals? Do you have the resources available? Can you make it happen by yourself? If not, who can help you?

"Media was very one way ... Now the internet is allowing what used to be a monologue to become a dialogue"

Joseph Gordon-Levitt

one minute wonder Be specific about what you want to achieve by marketing your business on social media. An increase in customers? Growth in market share? A rise in net profit? A jump in average order price per customer? Total revenue growth?

■ **R is for Realistic and Relevant to your business.** Do you need to do this? What will happen if you do? What will happen if you don't? What won't happen if you do or don't?

■ **T is for Time.** All good goals have a timeframe attached. Think about the long term and the short term. Then consider what is the easiest first step for you to take.

Create Specific, Measurable, Achievable, Realistic and Relevant goals with a Timeframe attached.

1.6

Stake a claim

The social media landscape is rather like the old Wild West gold-mining towns. There's definitely gold out there but if you don't put a stake in the ground to claim your territory then someone else will get there first and your brand is gone.

Once you have your brand make sure you start buying the websites, Twitter name, Tumblr accounts and blogs with the right name or names for your business and any products or topics you want to stake a claim to.

But even if you're not sure whether you are going to use a particular social media channel immediately, it is worth grabbing your place, especially with a new channel launch. The social media and digital worlds are so fast moving that a small channel may have hundreds of millions of users next year. If you've already got your brand name set up you won't need to worry about someone else taking it. Choose a consistent name across the channels, or if you have more than one brand, think through which channels are suitable for which brands.

Make sure you get your accounts 'verified' or authenticated where appropriate so that people know the accounts are real. You will notice on Twitter, for example, that verified accounts have a tick next to them.

one minute wonder Social media can be used as a way of reducing the costs of training staff. You can post videos and content online for your staff or run interactive seminars through apps like WizIQ. Interesting, interactive content will increase the learning experience.

The average user has more than one social media account and this number is likely to rise. However some users do still find a community they enjoy most and spend the majority of their time there. It's a complex situation for business. You need to know your users and also not spread yourself too thin.

Make sure you buy all the relevant account names you need before you begin, even if you don't use them immediately.

1.7

Draw up a content strategy

Free content is everywhere on the web. It's one of the biggest changes that the digital world has brought us. It is said that there is more information around in the last five years than in the whole of human history. Your content needs to make an impact to be noticed.

In the past people expected to pay for content. Now, users get it for free but they are still greedy for interesting new content every day.

Consider what products or services you are going to produce and promote. Then think how you can do this through interesting content that people will want to search for, print and save or forward to their friends.

Content can take the form of long or short blogs (posts about a particular subject, product or service), short tweets on Twitter, webinars, slideshares, photographs, videos on YouTube or Vine, e-books or infographics. This gives you a lot of scope for interesting, visual ways to present what you do.

Think about your three top products or services. Why would someone want them? How would they help them? What would make them buy them? Now think about how you can create three short pieces of writing which you can use as blog posts. Or perhaps you

"The first lesson of branding: memorability. It's very difficult buying something you can't remember" John Hegarty

one minute wonder When you are planning your content, only post when you can answer the three 'why' questions: Why this form of content? Why now? Why this channel? If your answers aren't clear then delay or ditch the idea and think again.

would like to write an e-book and promote it through ten or so regular blog posts that you post over a series of weeks?

There are so many choices. What about presenting the same information visually? How about laying it out as a PowerPoint? Or as a series of webinars? Would do you want to present? What if you could engage experts to present that information for you and interview them in a collection of videos? Perhaps you are going to present the information in multiple ways. Are you going to do it all at the same time or create anticipation by posting over a period of time?

You can present the same content in long blogs, short tweets, in photos or videos.

1.8

Be aligned

Social media is a two-way conversation. Part of it is driven from the 'bottom up' with millions of people all over the world active online. However, your approach to social media needs to be 'top down' – driven by a clear strategy – and aligned with the rest of your business.

Your social media strategy will only make an impact on your bottom line results by being part of your broader business plan. Once you have a clear idea of your brand you can create an overall marketing strategy and from that create a digital marketing campaign.

Your social media strategy sits within and alongside this marketing strategy. It should be aligned with your business rather than created in response to one specific social media platform. Of course, the digital world is very fast moving. Every day something is happening on social media and by the end of next year there will be new social media platforms you have never heard of. It's tempting to just act quickly every time a new app appears, but hold back and always keep aligned with your overall strategy. It is better to be a slow adopter of technology than to produce poor content that puts off potential customers.

one minute wonder Start by thinking about the top five sites which would be useful to you immediately. Then consider how you can achieve a balance between activity around sharing articles and expertise, product-centric posts, reviews, images and videos and how this all fits within your broader business strategy.

Have your brand strategy in place first before you begin your social media campaign.

1.9

Take an inventory

When someone clicks on your account on a social media channel you want them to find interesting content and keep browsing. Then you want them ideally to click on links to your website and other social media accounts. To achieve this you need to be interesting and relevant.

Do you have the knowhow and resources to post a lot of content frequently and consistently? You'll need to.

What content do you have available right now? Unless you are starting a business from scratch you probably already have a lot of content out there that is usable but just in the wrong form. Check for any existing videos about your organization, product or even employees. It doesn't matter if they are too long or dull for social media. You may be able to steal extracts or images and edit them into a different form. What about doing a mash-up of photos or bits of video to fun music?

Have you ever done any podcasts or written white papers? Have you taken photographs for annual reports or brochures? You probably already have more content than you realize. What about articles journalists have written about you? Do you have any testimonials from happy customers? Gather them all up.

one minute wonder Keep an ongoing database of your assets. Inventory them on a spreadsheet with headings divided up by topic and type, e.g. photograph, video, etc. Decide where you will use the content. Put an editorial calendar in place with clear deadlines.

Inventory your assets and see what you can revamp, edit and leverage into content for social media. If it is not suitable for now, simply archive it. Even that 1970s film of the employees in old-fashioned clothes may be fun to pull out for the anniversary of the founding of the company. You're only limited by your own creativity and imagination.

Inventory your assets and see what is usable for multimedia content.

1.10

Do it 24/7

Building a business costs money. At first glance social media looks appealing because it seems cheap. After all, many social media outlets like Instagram and Twitter cost nothing to set up an account. Others like LinkedIn charge for premium services but charge nothing for the basic registration.

If you are not paying in money, you do need to be prepared to pay in time. The first steps are easy. Open accounts under your name or your business name or under the name of the idea, product or service you want to promote.

However, it is not going to be enough to stick your name or business name all over the internet on lots of different sites and then leave them. You are going to need to keep active and investing time and effort, posting blogs, comments, tweets, pictures or videos. Be prepared to show people that it is worth their time paying you attention. If they pay with their attention you need to pay by keeping your accounts active again and again. If there is no regular activity people will have no reason to stick around.

Make sure you thoroughly assess your resources before you begin. Do you have the skills and resources within your company to put the time and effort needed into your social media strategy? It takes time to write content that your audience will want to click

one minute wonder Think about appointing someone who can spend time monitoring both positive and negative comments from your audience so that you can avoid problems and tailor your content to your audience. This person needs to be listened to at all levels of the organization so that your social media strategy is well integrated.

on and comment on. If they're interested in one piece of content they're going to want to hang around and look for related content. If you can't supply it, they'll soon find their way to someone who will.

■ **Focus on timing.** Between 8am and 8pm is peak time for posts being read.

■ **Be consistent.** Post several times a day (up to ten) on Twitter and frequently on other channels.

■ **Be broad.** Post across all your chosen social media channels.

Know your audience and invest the time to keep them happy.

Promote

Social media gives you access to hundreds of millions of customers. You can shape and share your brand on social media, creating a marketplace for minimum cost. However, to build a brand you need to create content and build connections with users so that you gain followers of your business.

2.1

Be sociable

The great thing about social media is that there are millions of people out there who want to talk as well as listen. These are the people who are going to help you to build your brand.

Social media is social. The clue's in the title. It's totally democratic. It allows anyone who can get onto the internet to have a conversation with anyone else. You can find areas of common interest with other people. You can meet a stranger in the virtual world and contribute to conversations, build social networks and participate in online communities.

To begin with it's exactly the same as meeting someone for the first time in person. You need to find something you can both have a conversation about. When the person you meet becomes interested in what you want to talk about, they're going to stay in touch with you.

case study One of the most effective brands of recent years has been Apple. Its great cutting-edge design and 'cool factor' has kept its customers loyal followers of the brand. Once someone buys an Apple they tend not to revert back to a PC but buy more and more of the Apple suite of products, upgrading and expand-

"Focus on how to be social, not on how to do social" Jay Baer

But after that it gets interesting. Social media is all about building communities and networks. You can build your relationships every day and turn a casual acquaintance into a fan or a follower very quickly. If one person becomes your fan they're likely to refer others to your account.

Make this happen by being social but with 'intent', working within your business strategy with one eye always on the end goal. Post content and start a conversation. You can post, make comments on a blog, or tweet a picture or video. Remember:

■ **Being social is being interactive.** You can have an immediate conversation with your customers but just like any conversation it needs to be a dialogue, not a monologue.

■ **Customers have an amazing choice of information and buying choices.** They now decide who they want to read about and listen to. Customers can't be *pulled* by business. They now *push* business to change.

■ **The tone of voice of business is changing.** You can still be an authority on your business but you'll need to adjust your mindset and chat rather than preach.

Interact with your customers and have real conversations.

ing what they own. From the beginning, Apple made design core to their brand, right down to the iconic apple logo at the back of the computer and the recognizable headphones. With every new product, people queue on the streets for hours to be the first to buy it. Apple owners have become 'brand citizens' of Apple.

2.2

Determine your ideal customer

Who is your audience? Who do you want as a customer? The more you know about your ideal customer the more you can promote your business effectively.

To begin, spend some time reviewing your existing customer base. This means asking yourself a lot of questions. What type of customer buys from you most often? Who spends most and who spends least? Which of your products are most popular with this type of customer? Is this your ideal type of customer or is there any attribute they lack? If so, what's stopping you having this type of customer now? Is there something you need to change about your business, products or services?

Now think about where you are most likely to find new customers like this. Where do they live? Does it matter? Are you limited by geography? Could you sell to a customer in Siberia, in Kenya or Alabama?

How could you attract more high-spending customers to your business through social media? What sort of content are they going to be interested in? Will they want to see photographs of what you do? Do you need to alert them to new product launches? Would

"Social media is about sociology and psychology more than technology" Brian Solis

one minute wonder A good exercise is to write a word picture of your ideal customer. Describe what they look like and their typical day. Where do they shop? Do they have children? What time do they get up? What do they watch on TV? It's rather like inventing a character for a book. The more you can visualize them the easier it will be to sell to them and to tailor the information you post to become an essential part of their busy lives.

they be interested in reading a blog? Do they belong to a particular profession? The more you can find out the more you can tailor your social media strategy effectively.

Get to know the profile of your ideal customer.

2.3

Convert the grazers

When you first start blogging and tweeting you'll be excited to attract grazers who touch down on your site and check you out. The internet is full of grazers. They are like flies at a picnic, flitting around, idly searching and seeing what is out there that might attract their attention. They may be drawn to your account by a keyword or phrase in your blog, a tweet that touches on their favourite subject or by a fun photo or video you posted.

Many people will follow a business for a day or so and get bored and move off to the next picnic rug to graze. Others will lurk around for a while, examine your website, scroll through your Twitter history, look through your followers and check out who you follow. They're basically deciding if you're their sort of person. Do they want to invest the time to follow you and click your posts, like your Facebook page and invest time in your brand? If they think they're interested they'll click the 'follow' button. However, they can easily 'unfollow' you as quickly as they followed you in the first place. It only takes seconds to follow or leave a site.

"The best marketing doesn't feel like marketing" **Tom Fishburne**

If you want to build a solid base of followers you'll need to give them not just one reason to follow your account but ten or a hundred reasons. It's not enough to open an account and post occasionally. You'll need to post interesting and consistent content and show them that if they link into your other accounts there are even more reasons to follow you. Then you have a chance of catching the grazers and turning them into followers for life.

Give your grazers a hundred reasons to stay and become a follower.

2.4

Build a community

Business can learn from the young. People shouldn't just buy your service or product or follow you or your business. Instead, they should see your brand as a community, a place they want to live in some of the time. You may be a citizen of a country. You can also become a citizen of a brand.

Teenagers have created some of the most loyal social media citizens on the web. They post videos on YouTube showing other teenagers how to do their makeup, what fashion to buy or how to deal with relationships. Their citizens feel as if they're personal friends with those they follow. Offline they'd queue for hours to see their idols.

Once you are part of a brand's community it means that you have loyalty to the brand, its values and what it wants to accomplish. This means as the brand owner you can get your followers to follow not only your core business but also other causes that you choose to support.

Winning citizens isn't the same as winning the odd follower. A citizen gets excited when they think about your brand. They feel proud to follow you. They feel in some way that you and your brand belong to them and they belong to you. You're their country and their tribe. In fact, they can't wait to tell other people about you. Big global brands evoke enormous loyalty among their customers. The best brands on social media understand this too. Their citizens contribute to the community because they also benefit from it.

"The best salespeople are not salespeople, they're people who've not only bought the product, but also bought into the idea of the company and the brand" Jarod Kintz

one minute wonder The best businesses really help their customers rather than just marketing and selling to them. Think back to your ideal customer. What does he or she most need in the world? What are their worries and concerns? How can you help ease their stresses? Perhaps you could post tips on how to save money? Or help them with easy recipes when they have no time after work? Think creatively.

Social media can be used for two purposes: to build social networks or online communities. A social network is a group of people you already know. An online community is formed out of groups of individuals who are held together by a common interest. Sometimes communities interact and overlap, even nesting within each other. Allow the space for online communities to form within your social media presence.

Think about creating brand citizens who feel as if they belong to your brand.

2.5

Become a friend

For many people online communities are now their communities. Virtual friends have replaced their friends in the real world. They spend significant amounts of time online chatting to people they have never met.

Your job is not to interrupt them and tell them about how great you and your organization are but to join in with their conversation and become one of them. You need to *look* and *sound* like someone they want to welcome into their existing community.

The way to do this is to sound like a human being. Talk as if you are talking to an individual, not to the mass market. This is where social media feels very different from old media and traditional marketing. Traditional marketing is designed for mass consumption but with social media marketing you need to make sure that individuals feel that you are talking directly to them as a friend or peer.

case study Sites like BuzzFeed have become hugely successful and influential because they have tapped into this human side. They specialize in creating lists that get people talking. These lists get talked about

> # "If you want to understand how a lion hunts, don't go to the zoo. Go to the jungle"
> **Jim Stengel**

For example, you wouldn't interrupt a conversation at a party and start describing the design specifications of the new car you are making, would you? Of course not. So don't do it on social media. But you might share a joke at a party or talk about the latest film you saw. So how about sharing a fun video online of two cars racing each other and yours winning? Or what about a moody shot of your car driving into a beautiful landscape? Why not provide a link to an article about how people can save money by choosing a car with good fuel economy? Perhaps you can even get your community of followers to do the work for you and ask them to name your new car. Don't be just a business. Be an interesting friend.

Remember, anyone can join any community. If people are choosing to join yours make sure you're as good a friend as they would find in their individual social networks.

Ditch the marketing jargon and hard sales and learn to talk 'human'.

and shared around. Most of all they create a feeling of belonging to the BuzzFeed brand. Every day people check in to find the next list they can share.

2.6

Inspire

This is your chance to create some thing magical and/or meaningful. Be a bit different. Have fun, set the bar high and set yourself apart. You don't need to spend a lot of money. You just need to use your imagination.

If you really want to create fans, followers and friends you need to invest in creating deep and lasting connections. It is not going to be enough to post tweets about how great your new accounting service is or to blog about your new slimming food range (even if your blog has lots of beautifully chosen pictures).

Ultimately people can pick and choose where they go on the web. In seconds. They don't need to hang around.

Add value but also inspire. Show how your organization can help your ideal customer to achieve the lifestyle they want, save money, make their home more beautiful or just feel good about themselves. The content should make them feel something – joy, happiness, success, fulfilment and a sense of belonging. By focusing on creating feelings in your audience through your content, you will get people to feel a deep sense of connection in return. Even a one-person band can do this, as the success of all the young YouTube users shows.

one minute wonder Create an online vision board using your products. Engage a designer to show your products as part of a desirable lifestyle. You can show how the vision board can be adapted with different colours; for example, for different demographics.

When you begin writing and posting content, think about who you can inspire today. The whole family? Parents? Children? Grandparents? Can your business help them build a better future or help them with real concerns or problems they have today? We don't just like those who inspire us. We love them.

Create valuable content, not just pretty pictures and platitudes.

Post

Different social media sites differ in the types of users they attract and the tone of voice and length and type of content. Some are more formal. Some are less so. Some have opportunities for paid content. Others stay free. Consider how you want to position your business and the benefits and disadvantages of different channels.

3.1

Start a blog

A blog can be a standalone place on the web where you promote your business or be integrated into your main website. You can use your blog to publish pieces about a particular subject and add regular value. You can have one blog site for a business or several for different purposes and different employees.

Start by setting up your blog sites and decide what you are going to write about. If you are a one-person band it doesn't have to be expensive to create a blog. There are many sites such as WordPress where you can create a well-presented blog in minutes for no charge.

■ You can post daily or weekly blogs on a particular theme or updates on industry news. You may want to post standalone content at first or link promotions.
■ Even on the simplest blogs you can add photos or other imagery to make your blog stand out and look attractive. Why not spend time gathering some interesting images?
■ Encourage comments from the beginning – if no one is noticing your blog then make sure you highlight the latest post on your Facebook or Twitter feed.

"Submit your brand to the general public. Your brand may be well made, but it has to be well known" Israelmore Ayivor

one minute wonder For a fee you can often add more graphics, visuals and other features to your blog. Think about how the visual look of your blog is going to fit into your overall social media strategy. Is it worth commissioning some graphics and a professional photo that you can also use on other channels?

The great thing about having a blog is that you can create fresh, readable content and even link with other blogs. Share your blogs widely and encourage others to share. By allowing comments on your blog you can increase activity and get noticed by Google, which will drive even more users to your site. Make sure that you have a clear editorial calendar so that you keep a check on what you are posting and when. Writing a number of blogs in advance can be an efficient use of time.

Write some blogs in advance which you can post at regular intervals.

3.2

Tweet

It doesn't take that long to become an expert tweeter. Whether you are a one-person band or an international blue-chip, you can run a Twitter account and actively tweet every day. Unlike some social media networks, like Facebook, where the default setting is to ask for permission to gain access to someone, on Twitter you can tweet someone in any country. You can, of course, set your profile to private or block a follower but the majority of accounts don't do this. Twitter is all about attracting large numbers of followers.

Twitter is one of the easiest social media platforms for growing your brand. All you need to do is to sign up with a name, a byline/bio for your profile and a photograph. Remember to put your website and Facebook page, LinkedIn page or other details as part of your bio. You can also set other social media apps so they automatically post to Twitter.

Use Twitter to network and build connections. Start by following other accounts. By the time you get to over a hundred you'll get a sense of what's going on around the Twittersphere 24 hours a day. Of course, you don't need to follow that many accounts. You could just

"Social media is a conversation, not a message"
Anon

> **one minute wonder** You can use Twitter for internal marketing, i.e. talking to colleagues. If you want to keep things private use the direct message facility, but it's OK to have more personal conversations visible on your tweet history as long as you strike a balance.

start tweeting yourself or retweeting interesting tweets that are relevant to your business. However, one of the benefits of following is that it gets you noticed and soon you should get followed back.

Share news and content and build awareness about your business and any marketing campaign. You'll soon notice the benefits of having real-time conversations with your customers, staff, friends and others. Listen to how many people are talking about your brand. Are they being positive or negative? Make sure you reply to tweets and get a conversation going.

Use Twitter to build connections, share company news and build awareness of your marketing campaign.

3.3

Create a Facebook page

Facebook is a global network where you can regularly update your friends on what is going on in your life. Most young and middle-aged people in your marketplace are likely to have an account. They post updates and photos on their lives and share links to things, places, videos, services and ideas they like. Facebook may have started as a place for friends and family but businesses are increasingly seeing the advantage of having a Facebook page.

■ Create a page for your business and post updates and photos that people can 'like'. Post about your products regularly as well as generic news.

■ Make sure you give your customers a reason to link to your Facebook page by posting images and videos as well as written content. Remember, again it is not about selling. It's about creating a community.

■ Set clear rules for content. Keep an eye on what is posted and make sure no users of your page write anything that is libellous or inappropriate.

"Facebook Fan Pages are email newsletters with smaller pictures" Jay Baer

one minute wonder Through Facebook Connect you can get people to connect with you from another website without the need to create an account or have a password. This tool instantly links two accounts.

■ If you can get a visitor to your page to fill in a survey, they will engage more with you and spend more time at your site.

■ Why not run a competition? You don't have to offer a huge prize. You'll find lots of people just enjoy the challenge of taking part and the glory of winning.

■ Don't wait for comments. Start a discussion by asking a question or posing a challenge.

Every Facebook fan you have has his or her own special network. If you make their experience enjoyable they are likely to refer their social network to your Facebook page.

Create a page on Facebook and post regular updates on your activities.

3.4

Link in

LinkedIn is a social media channel where professionals can post a version of their CV and link up with other professionals. It works on the theory of six degrees of separation: I can reach pretty much anybody else in the world by using six connections. Social networks are characterized by a spider web-like structure. The inner ring consists of people you know. The outer rings are people they know.

Suppose I start by signing up a hundred contacts I know personally (my 1st-degree contacts); their friends (my 2nd-degree contacts) may number thousands. By the time I reach my 3rd-degree contacts (the friends of friends' friends) I may be up to the million mark in multiple countries.

Research shows that people are more likely to find a job via the friend of a friend rather than directly from someone they know, and LinkedIn is a great means of networking to get a new career. However, the networking principle works just as well for businesses. If my network stretches across the globe, in theory I can find someone who can help me to look for new employees without paying an agent, or just get information. Perhaps I need to find a salesperson in China but my business is based in America. No problem. What if I need a new

one minute wonder Make sure you ask for a minimum of three recommendations on LinkedIn. You can ask for a recommendation from any contact you are linked in to. However, avoid mutually endorsing them as this will undermine their recommendation.

non-executive director for my board? No problem again. I can search directly or via my network.

On LinkedIn you can start a page for your company or create a group around a subject. You can connect with other users by posting interesting links on topics or by participating in discussions with other groups. The more contacts you create the easier it will be to find whoever you want whenever you need to.

Consider creating a business page on LinkedIn as well as a personal profile.

3.5

Video it

Who would have thought that a video of a South Korean singer could attract millions of viewers outside his own country? Yet the combination of 'Gangnam Style' and YouTube made Psy into an international star.

Easily accessible online video made the difference. On TV, a programme is shown once and if you're lucky gets repeated or can be viewed for a short time on a catch-up service. In contrast, a video posted on YouTube can go viral in seconds and then stays there gathering viewers.

YouTube and other video-sharing channels have an additional attraction. People can now find the most obscure interests catered for in a way they never were in the past. Do you want to see objects broken up and filmed in slow motion? You can now. Do you need a five-minute Buddhist meditation to listen to? It's there. How about advice on your

case study The British retailer John Lewis specializes in creating beautiful Christmas adverts every year with specially commissioned music. Over the last few years they have garnered millions of extra viewers by posting their videos on YouTube. Users share the links via Twitter as they would a new pop video. In 2014 they

diet, a new makeup regime, or instructions on how to repair a broken toilet seat? All these and many, many more can be found on the web. Of course, some videos have millions of viewers and some have fewer than ten but it is clear that there is a vast audience out there if you can find something useful, interesting or simply funny to post on the web.

Why not post useful how-to guides, beautiful adverts or even charity fundraisers linked to your business? A video doesn't even need to be long. Vine is a social media channel where videos of just a few seconds can be shared between users. It has been hugely successful. On Snapchat you can share a photo or video and it disappears after viewing. Apps like Meercat and Periscope allow live video streaming.

Video can be used for long-lasting promotion or viral marketing.

created a heartfelt video about a boy and his toy penguin with specially commissioned music to accompany it. Soon the #MontyThePenguin hashtag was being shared on Twitter and the video was gaining millions of views on social media before and at the same time as being shown on TV.

3.6

Share slides

If you've created a great presentation that would benefit others, why not share it by posting it online on a site like SlideShare?

SlideShare has many positive points for businesses. There is far less competition on a site like SlideShare compared to the bigger multimedia sites. This means it's easier to get noticed on the site even though there are millions of users. You can grow your followers by targeting your presentations at a very specific audience and also can get email subscribers. SlideShare also features some new presentations on their home page each day, so make sure you get yours online early enough so it has a chance of being picked.

However, you have to start by constructing a great presentation. There are three things you must remember:

1 **Topic.** Pick an interesting topic and give it a shocking, exciting, standout title that grabs attention. Your title is the hook that is going to land you a reader.

2 **Be logical.** You need a clear structure for your presentation. One popular structure is to have seven main points. Another is to construct a list with a slide for each item.

3 **Visuals.** Your slides need to be well designed with interesting visuals. Most people upload dull-looking slides and don't even use colour. So make sure you use colour and graphics.

Now, make sure that people can find your presentation through searching online by adding the right keywords and phrases. You can post a link to your presentation on LinkedIn. This channel is an obvious choice for posting business presentations because the professionals who use the site are particularly interested in sector-related topics. You can share it on Facebook, Twitter and Pinterest as well. You can even embed the presentation on your blog.

Embed your presentation on your blog so it is easy to find.

3.7

Instagram it

Sites like Instagram are popular because they allow users to post images of anything they are interested in. Instagram can act as a great shop window for your product. But even if you don't have a physical product to sell, you can still use it to market your service.

Here are six ways you can use Instagram to help your business grow:

1 Show pictures of your products. Photograph the finished product. Show it from different angles, in different settings, or even photographed in an arty or unusual way.

2 Show the place where you do business. How about photographing your office, factory or even the production line? Show the route from concept to product.

3 Show the people who make your business happen. Give your audience a sneak peek behind the scenes.

4 Come up with examples of how people can use your product or service. You can even ask for users to post their pictures of them using your product.

one minute wonder How about getting interest for the book you are writing for your business by posting pictures that link with the theme of the book? You could even run a competition and ask your followers to guess the name of the book based on the pictures.

5 How about showing a day in the life of the boss? Post photos of what happened when you took that sales trip to China or visited your factory in Russia.

6 Add a touch of glamour to your brand. Share pictures of celebrities carrying your new handbag or on the slopes using the skis you make or drinking wine from your vineyard.

Think about creative ways you can present images of your business on Instagram.

3.8

Blog on Tumblr

There are over 200 million blogs on Tumblr. Tumblr is a social networking site which sits between a blogging and a micro-blogging platform. It has some of the best features of Twitter and WordPress put together. You can write posts on Tumblr and share photos and videos. It is free and versatile with a timeline feature.

When you open a Tumblr account you will need to set up a primary blog where you can post and follow other users. You can then, if you wish, open secondary blogs and even allow users to be administrators on them. Choose an appealing name for your blog, e.g. 'Home-brewed beer', and start posting. Watch as the number of followers grows!

■ **Text posts.** The simplest form of post is text only, with or without a title. When you are in a hurry do a quick update on your blog in text only.

■ **Chats.** Create a title and a chat post where you can start a conversation, e.g. 'Does anyone know what beer goes best with blue cheese?'

■ **Links.** Add some links by posting a title and caption, e.g. 'Pubs' and 'Best pub in Scotland', then a link to the relevant website.

one minute wonder Showcase your organization with great graphics. Tumblr is very visual. You can choose visual themes from more than a thousand themes (either free or paid for). You can even create your own theme which is very useful for any business where aesthetics are important.

■ **Photographs.** Upload your chosen images with a caption e.g. 'Our newest beer, hot from the brewery'. You can add more than one photo. Watch it go viral.

■ **Videos.** Remember videos don't need to be serious. How about uploading a video of your employees dancing to Beyonce? You can add links to other video sharing sites, too.

■ **Audio.** Think about adding interviews about your product or how about a few tracks of music that go well with beer?

■ **Stories.** Writers and graphic artists use Tumblr to build their portfolios online with text and pictures.

Tumblr is one of the best platforms on which to get a marketing campaign to go viral.

3.9

Pin it on Pinterest

Pinterest works like a digital version of an old-fashioned pinboard. You can create a board around any topic you choose and post or 'pin' text or images around your topic. Because it is very well suited to imagery, you can create a collection of pictures for your board.

Make sure you research what your competitors are doing on Pinterest. See if there are any new ways you can create a profile with personality and post some interesting topics.

How could it work for your business? Let's say you are a pasta specialist. You could use Pinterest to showcase beautiful pictures of pasta dishes with recipes attached or maybe even the ideal setting in Italy to eat your pasta. You can pin prices to your pictures and there are stronger click-through and conversion rates to sales than on some other sites.

Or perhaps you are a landscape gardener. Why not put together some vision boards with ideas for garden designs, unusual plants or the latest fashions in garden furniture as a showcase for your work and credibility?

Of course, you can post text and images on other sites but as a high of percentage of Pinterest users are female, it provides a different demographic from other channels. Pinterest users appear to be particularly interested in areas such as crafts, DIY, fashion and cookery, so if you are in any of these areas you should definitely consider a Pinterest blog. Make sure you like and comment on other boards to grow your Pinterest community.

Create beautiful vision boards on Pinterest to inspire your customers.

Position

It's great to get noticed by a lot of people once for something you posted but the aim of using social media is to build sustained relationships that keep your business going over years, not days. How you position yourself for the long term is vital to how successfully you build your web influence.

4.1

Lead opinion

Some companies seem to think that social media is just about networking. If all you want is to reach out to your industry peers then that's fine. But to really get yourself noticed you need to become a leader of opinion. Then you'll be trusted as a source to come back to again and again.

The world has become information savvy and social media is highly meritocratic. If you're interesting enough you will get noticed. If you are boring you won't. People are looking for the best content presented in the most interesting, informative or entertaining way. Social media is your chance to get ahead of the competition.

■ **Get noticed.** Create content that is attention grabbing and visually interesting on different platforms to drive traffic to your main business website or blog.

■ **Be an expert.** Speak with authority on topics of interest to your core users. Make sure your audience learns something new or sees things from a new angle.

■ **Be a knowledge hub.** Provide links to other experts' whitepapers, retweet interesting tweets from experts in the field.

■ **Keep current.** Always make sure you stay on brand, stay current, relevant and interesting.

"Content builds relationships. Relationships are built on trust. Trust drives revenue"

Andrew Davis

one minute wonder Think about how you can add value to people's lives. It is not enough to make friends. You are trying to create an image for your business. Allow comments on your blog, respond to tweets and questions on Facebook. Be helpful and be informative. Become an invaluable part of the social media community.

■ Participate in discussions. Keep the topic going by adding updates, new posts, links and relevant comments.

Being an opinion leader creates a stronger brand by getting people to think of you as a trusted peer rather than a corporation that is trying to sell something.

Make yourself into an opinion leader and a trusted peer.

4.2

Have values

Simply put, a value is something that matters to you. We all have different values as individuals. Groups, communities and even countries have different values. Companies do, too.

Some of these values are very obvious – for example, you may value efficiency and honesty in your company and that is clear to every employee from the person who cleans the office to the CEO. However, you may take other values for granted and assume that everybody knows them but they may not be obvious to everyone. This is very common in many organizations.

As an example: imagine a private care home organization where the CEO's main goal for the business is to make money. Further down the organization, where the employees come into contact with their customers, they value helping people above saving costs or making profits. Who speaks for the brand of the business when there is a clash of values? You'll end up not only with problems with staff but also an unclear understanding of the brand of the business from customers.

Whoever writes and posts your social media content needs to be clear about all of the values of your business. Otherwise your followers will pick up on values of the person who is doing the posting, which may not be the same as the values of the business.

one minute wonder Create a list of values. Begin by asking yourself what is most important to you as a business. Next, dig a little deeper about what these values mean specifically to you. For example, if you write down, 'being an expert', what does that mean to you? Precise language will get you better business results. Finally, rank your values from one to ten. What are the top values?

Even if you are a one-person band, still take the time to sit down and work out what's important to you. Now think about how you can get those values across in your writing.

Ask yourself the question, 'What's important to this business?'

4.3

Look consistent

Every contact and every impression counts on the web. Some impressions are conscious but many more will be unconscious. They will be positive, negative or neutral and obviously you want to leave a positive impression. A consistent look to your brand makes you look trustworthy.

Since each different social media channel has their own look and feel you need to think carefully about how you are going to create consistency across all the channels you use. What image do you want to promote to your customers online? Consistency doesn't mean you need to be boring. It is perfectly possible to have a personality and be consistent. However, everything must relate back to your brand and brand promise. There is no point creating a humorous profile on one site and a serious corporate one on another.

■ Think about the colours you use in your website or blog – the sort of images that best reflect your business. Colours should be consistent.
■ Consider your bio and profiles. Are you going to promote your business through one person or through the company name?
■ Choose words carefully, e.g. if you are going to write a Million one time, MLLN the next and MN the time after, it will just look sloppy.

■ Invest time and money in a strong logo. It musn't distract but should be strong enough to support the brand and fit in with the rest of the design.

■ Limit yourself to a maximum of three fonts. Any more is distracting and can overpower the rest of your design.

■ The pictures you choose should reflect the personality of your brand. Think: if the brand were a person, what sort of activities would it do?

Be consistent in the look you create across different channels.

4.4

Have a tone of voice

Tone of voice is a term used in marketing to describe the personality of a business that comes through the written word. When you read a piece of writing you get a sense of the voice and personality of the person behind it.

Think about something you have read online recently. What impression did it leave you with about the person who wrote it? Were they funny, shy, authoritative, dull, bold, cheeky? Now have a look on Twitter. Read a few posts and see what impression you get of the writer, without looking at their photo or profile.

It's amazing, isn't it, how quickly we think we know somebody from just a few words? Language is very powerful. You are influenced by the length of words people use, whether they choose jargon, or abbreviate often, even by the use of 'it's' rather than 'it is' or by whether they address you directly as 'you' rather than 'the reader' or 'the user'.

What is your personality? How could this be reflected in the tone of voice of your writing? Consider how you want to sound. Light-hearted? Happy? Warm? Friendly?

Flick through magazines and newspapers as well as blogs and Twitter feeds. Notice the sort of words people use to create an impression? When you start to write your content, keep an awareness of how you will sound to the person reading.

"Audience engagement is critical to the survival of your brand" Bernard Kelvin Clive

one minute wonder Make a list of all the common jargon in use in your organization and business sector. Consider whether these are words that your audience will understand or whether they sound too formal or alienating. If so, come up with a list of simple substitutes.

■ **Do updates.** If you edit or make changes on one channel, make sure you do the same on your other channels at the same time.

Think about the tone of voice that fits the personality of your organization.

4.5

Use professionals

Not everyone is a great photographer, a great writer or knows how to direct a professional video. You may think you're saving a ton of money if you do everything on social media yourself, but you may just end up sabotaging the reputation of your organization in a very public way.

If you don't know how to do it, don't waste time trying to learn it. Buy in a great freelance writer. Hire a fantastic editor. Engage an agency which specializes in social media or digital marketing. Work with a partner who can do all your Photoshop for you. Then make sure they are fully on board with your goals and understand your brand.

There are lots of people out there to choose from, so make sure you take your time and don't just go with the cheapest. If they are good, they are going to ask lots of questions about your brand rather than just come up with a fancy design for your website. Find out who they work for already. Ask what size of projects they deal with and what they won't do as well as what they will do. Content? Design? Editing? Brand development?

Having a great social media presence is not something you do once and forget about. It's a journey you will take probably with partners in tow. There are lots of freelancers out there all over the world who talk the talk but aren't going to stick with you for the long term. Choose wisely.

"Clients don't care about the labor pains; they want to see the baby" **Tim Williams,** *Ignition*

one minute wonder Make sure that you create a brand guide for any freelance writers you hire. They should be able to understand your brand and the tone of voice you expect them to write in as well as how this will fit into the overall look of your brand.

Think about what you can't do in-house and think about taking on partners.

4.6

Google well

When you write your first blog the first thing you want is for someone to notice you. Nowadays if a blog doesn't pop up on Google it might as well not exist. Twitter and Facebook accounts will show up under your name on Google but if your main social media marketing channel is your blog you need to work to get it noticed. Even though blogs get noticed more than a static website, users are going to find your blog either through links from your website, social media accounts or through searching. Google searches regularly for new sites using its 'spider' software, but that's not enough.

Use keywords. Keywords are search terms that direct search engines like Google or Yahoo towards you. It is pointless just having captions and photographs on your primary blog. Google's spider crawls around the web looking for words as reference. Write a piece of text describing what your business does, e.g. private dentist based in Manchester, and Google will find you more quickly. Remember it is better to be as specific as possible, e.g. 'nutritionist working with children', rather than nutritionist.

"Google only loves you when everyone else loves you first"

Wendy Piersall

one minute wonder Why not create a video on YouTube talking about your new blog? Make sure you post a link to the blog and your main website as well as a description of what the video is about. You can also tweet about it. Or how about using one of the new live video channels like Periscope to film short, more spontaneous-looking videos? This allows you to see instantly who is watching you.

Link to other quality websites, post a guest post to your blog so that it links to their blog. Link to other articles of interest to your audience or to article directories. This will all help to build links to your blog. You can also submit your blog to a blog directory which will help to expand the number of links you attract.

Add your blog link to other social media profiles and share it by posting status updates on your Facebook page or on Twitter. This will alert Google. You can also pay Google for optimum status for your blog.

Think about what keywords will attract visitors to your blog.

4.7

Network offline

Social media is not a magic wand. All your efforts will be wasted if you don't spend time networking and building your business offline at the same time. The customers you add offline can provide testimonials for the customers online. So get out and get networking in the real world. Every new person can make connections for you and add money to your results.

Your social media presence works in more than one way. It serves as a showcase for your business and hopefully gets people to be interested enough to link through to your website and buy something, or pick up the phone and ask for help.

When you meet people in a day-to-day business setting, social media acts as a credibility check. One of the first things they are going to do when they get back to the office is to check out your online presence. What are you talking about on Twitter? Do you have any interesting blogs on Tumblr? Have you written an e-book on that topic you referred to over lunch? They may even check you out on their smartphone when you go off to pay the bill. If your social media presence doesn't fit with the story you've been telling, then you may lose the contact or even the deal.

one minute wonder The old-fashioned business card is a cheap way to get you followers online. As well as an address, add your account names and make sure anyone who has your account can find your Facebook, Twitter, LinkedIn and other channel pages easily.

It pays to invest time in networking, whether you are online or offline.

Monitor

Once you have set up a social media presence it's important to keep in touch with how well it's working. Factor in time to read feedback, view the numbers regularly and respond to your posts. Use professional tools to save time and be organized.

5.1

Listen and learn

Businesses are great at broadcasting but not always great at listening. With social media they need to be.

A growing number of consumers access social media platforms on the go throughout the day through their mobile phones. When they post a comment on a blog or on Twitter it's as easy as texting a friend. Young mobile users are enthusiastic and engaged. They expect to be listened to and answered when they post a comment as quickly as when their friend replies to a text. And remember, if you've got your brand right, you aren't just a business, you're one of them; a friend.

When you listen and learn from your followers there will be many benefits for your business:

■ You'll gain market knowledge and insight into your customers, learning what they like, what they don't like and what services and products they value enough to pay for.
■ You'll enhance their brand experience and gain their loyalty. They'll come back again and again.
■ Your reputation will be boosted. You'll become the place where people come to get answers and chat.
■ You'll create sales and marketing efficiency and effectiveness; boosting your return on your investment of time and money.

"We were given two ears and one mouth for a reason" Anon

one minute wonder First research and find your potential audience. Understand what they want. Who is giving it to them now? Perhaps no one? Target your audience. Market directly to them. Convert them to brand citizens by giving them what they want.

You can learn through feedback how to improve your product, brand, processes and services. You may even pick up technical tips from your customers.

Don't just put content out there, read the comments.

5.2

Monitor

Social media gives you valuable data to measure your marketing success. You can monitor how many people have liked your blog page, which of them has looked at your LinkedIn page and when and how many hits you are getting on Google.

What you really want to find out is your followers' level of involvement with your brand. Are your numbers growing, declining or stable? This isn't as simple as it seems. Some users will disappear for a while and then return days, weeks or months later; however, over a period of time you will be able to get a good idea of how you are seen online.

Involvement = I + I + I + I:

■ **Interaction.** Do users react to what you post and how much do they interact with it? Do they follow you on more than one social media channel, interact regularly or inconsistently?

■ **Impact.** Pay close attention to how many of your followers convert to become paying customers. If they do, how long does it take them to do so? If they don't buy, why not? What would it take to make them pay for your product or service?

one minute wonder Take the time to work out the lifetime value of a new customer for your organization based on your existing data. As you begin to use social media, pay attention to your customer retention rate and to how many new customers are coming to you via social media.

◖ Influence. Are your followers talking about your business and recommending it to other people? Do your products get mentioned in their posts? If not, why not?

◖ Inspiration. Have you inspired anyone to share anything creative or different that will get you talked about in a positive way?

Think carefully about how much you can and should tailor your interactions on social media to take account of the different personalities and profiles of your customers. Make sure you stay aligned with your core brand and don't lose the core of who you are as a business in an effort to win new customers.

Monitor how your followers react to what you post.

5.3

Use surveys

Surveys are a very effective tool to use in your socia
media strategy. They provide you with a great way
to get to know your audience. Think about why you
want to survey your audience. You might want to
find out their views on your products, how they use
social media, what they think of your blogs, wha
groups they belong to or which channels they visi
most frequently. You may be surprised at their
answers.

You can post a short survey to your website, blog or a channe
such as Facebook using a tool like SurveyMonkey.

■ Make sure your audience knows why it is worthwhile to participate
Say what the survey's about and provide an incentive to take part.
■ Aim your survey at a particular group your followers can identif
with, such as 'voters', 'cake eaters', 'fantasy-fiction fans'. Describe th
survey as being of benefit to this group.
■ Ask them to do it now. Suggest a time by which they need to
complete the survey. Let them know how many minutes it will take
to complete.

"Sell-sell-sell sales methods simply do not work on social media" Kim Garst

one minute wonder Ask your followers to forward the link to your survey so that you can reach a larger number of people. Schedule automatic reminders to be sent to your network while the survey is open to make sure as many people as possible fill it in. Thank them for filling in your survey and if you can, show them the results as they change.

Use positive language to describe what you want your audience to do. For example, 'Hello, crime-fiction fans. Tell us what you think about our new crime-fiction review site today. We'd love you to share your views with us right now/today. Please complete our survey {LINK}'.

The information you want to find out may vary from channel to channel. Think about changing the questions you ask to suit the channel or think about running a number of more regular surveys with only one or two questions to avoid survey fatigue.

Show your followers why it will benefit them to complete your survey.

5.4

Use hashtags

Another way to gather views and feedback or promote an idea, product or service is to use hashtags on Twitter. A hashtag looks like this #.

If you look at Twitter you will see that popular subjects have a hashtag sign followed by a word, abbreviation or several words. Hashtags can be used to describe the name of a TV programme, a book, an idea or a topic that people want to trend on Twitter, e.g. #justsaying. People who are interested in a particular topic will monitor Twitter.

Think about your question and either ask it with an appropriate hashtag added or add a specific invitation link to fill in a survey or participate in a vote on a topic. Here are some types of hashtags you can use:

case study June was a first-time user of Twitter. She was interested in setting up a business as a freelance publisher specializing in romantic fiction. After setting up an account on Twitter with a profile talking about her interests, she searched for any hashtags with the phrase 'romantic fiction' in them and then began to

Specific topics. To get views on a topic, e.g. the latest election, simply use the hashtag #Juneelection so that people following the election can find you. Monitor what people tweet.

Conference. Gather the views of participants about how the latest conference went. Use a hashtag like #ABCcompanyconference2019 to disseminate news and gather views from the attendees.

Product/Service launch. Use a hashtag like #newABCcar to find out what people think about the design of your new product or service.

Groups or organizations. Target a particular group of people or members of a particular profession to ask them their views with hashtags like #Texandoctors or #HRprofessionalsUK.

Video. Promote your YouTube video of your newly launched car and get people's opinions on it with a hashtag such as #fastestcarinthewest.

Hashtags on Twitter can get a response in seconds.

find people who were interested in the same area as her. She built up a group of followers very quickly, getting noticed by posting regularly and engaging with her followers using hashtags to get her posts noticed.

5.5

Find the influencers

Wouldn't it be great if you had people singing your praises every day? While getting the approval of any customer is great for your brand, getting the approval of influential people is even better.

■ Identify the key influencers in your follower network as well as any influencers in the wider media who could give a valuable endorsement to you, your business or product.

■ Check out the influencer's reputation and their social media profile. Does it fit with your brand? Their reputation will become your reputation. Use the @ tag to tweet them and see if they notice you.

■ Build your influencer network before you need it. Make them part of your brand community by making your approach personal. Be warm and friendly.

■ Write about them, interview them, invite them on to your channel. Give to them and they will want to reciprocate.

■ Offer them free samples of your product. Ask them to write a review on your blog or be interviewed on a podcast talking about your product.

one minute wonder Ask your followers to send their questions or topics to be discussed and host a Twitter interview with the influencer you are interested in. They will be impressed that you already have an active community of followers and fans and will see the benefits of converting your followers into their followers.

You don't need to stick to written content. If you are just starting out but know your app is going to be the one to beat, identify vloggers on YouTube in your area with large numbers of followers and suggest that they give their opinion on your product. This kind of strategy promotes authentic conversations that social media users enjoy even if they know the products are being promoted.

Identify your influencers and ask them to review your products.

5.6

Use professional tools

Many sites like Tumblr or WordPress use a tool called a dashboard. On your dashboard you can see the number of followers you have and who you are following.

It is easy on some social media platforms like WordPress or LinkedIn to keep an eye on trends in followers and likes, but if you want to become a real expert there are also a number of more specialist measurement tools around that will help you to keep an eye on the reach of your message. These include tools like Crowdbooster, Simply Measured and Demographics Pro. You can also find tools which monitor social conversations and act as content distribution tools. These include Buffer, Hootsuite, Buddy Media and Meshfire.

Finally, listening tools help you to get customer insights about customer sentiment by analysing conversations on social media. Take a look at Radian6, Vocus, Sysomos and Topsy.

By using specialist monitoring tools you can take apart all the data generated by social media platforms and become much more responsive to what's happening out there. It doesn't mean you have to just be reactive either. When you really start to understand your customer and how they feel about you, you can use some of those tools to produce content across the social media platforms you are on.

one minute wonder Entertain your followers by creating collages using an app like Layout or Photogrid. You can post your collages to a social media site like Facebook or Instagram. Get everyone involved by asking them for their collages around a particular theme or subject.

Of course, not all these tools are suitable for every size of business since they vary in terms of how much they are going to cost. So take a look first at what is available for free on the social platforms you are on and consider carefully whether you need to go the next step up.

Use free and paid-for tools to monitor and measure the impact of your social media.

Be real

Stand out from the crowd by having a personality. No one has to read your blogs or tweets or like your Facebook page. They will do it only if they enjoy them or find them useful. Write like a human being, have real conversations and you'll soon make an impact.

6.1

Be authentic

Your followers want you to be human whether you are a one-person business or a big organization. They want to know there's a real person there behind the words and the logo.

You don't always need to share a whole load of personal information. I don't need to know when you had a shower this morning or what you had for breakfast but I do want you to seem like a real person.

Start with the basics. Speak human. Who wants to read a tweet or a blog full of words like 'blue sky thinking' or the latest piece of management speak? Avoid jargon. Write as you would to a friend or family member. If you are listening to your followers you will soon get to know what they are like and what they enjoy and don't like, just as you would with a friend.

Be transparent. If someone asks you a question, answer it. We like people who answer questions directly and tell us something real about themselves.

Share what you can share unless it is a state secret or will harm your business. It is nice to see what goes on behind the scenes. We don't always need to see the perfected product. Why not show the potato that never made it as far as the supermarket or what happened when the office ceiling fell in?

one minute wonder Develop your own checklist to make sure you don't cross any lines. Some good questions to start with are: How much and what should I share, and with whom? How do I know if this is too much? Do people really want to know what I had for breakfast? Am I giving away too much to the competition?

Be human and speak human by talking to followers as real people.

6.2

Get feedback and endorsements

Let's suppose you have a new cleaning product that is about to come on the market. Or perhaps you're trying to challenge the leaders in your market to produce the best cat food. Social media gives you an opportunity to gather lots of opinions about your products and make them great.

In the old days, one of the only ways a business could get feedback would be to set up a market research focus group and use a professional to test opinion and feed it back to the company. While paying for research may be feasible for big businesses it can be too expensive for many small ones.

But now you can find out what people think with very little effort. You can reach both existing product users and potential users. Reach out

case study The Deliciously Ella blog focuses on healthy food choices. Ella Woodward, the blogger, has gained thousands of followers by sharing not only her recipes but also her reason for starting the blog. She talks about how she dealt with her health problems

to your network and ask your followers what they think about your new product or even the old product they have used for years.

People love to give their opinions and if you're asking them on Twitter or Facebook they're pretty sure you are listening, which makes them more likely to give you what you want. This kind of feedback is invaluable as it is as near to real-time feedback as you are ever likely to get. It's much cheaper than running a market research group and even quicker than an emailed or mailed survey.

Ask for feedback on your new product and save money on focus groups.

by changing her eating habits. Sharing her story helps others along the same journey to improved eating. Now she has published a recipe book which was serialized in a national newspaper.

6.3

Go off topic

Writing content for the web isn't like writing a textbook. No one has to read what you have written and even if you are the cleverest person in the room it's easy to bore your followers.

You'll seem more like a real person rather than a faceless company if now and then you go off topic. Of course, some people may follow you just to get an update about your latest discounts or to be the first to get hold of your new product, but even they are going to get bored if that's all that's happening. Or, even worse, if they get the same marketing tweet 50 times a day.

Think about posting something fun. You can choose something that's not necessarily directly connected to your business but that you can make a feature of. For example, Google often changes the visual image for Google on their search engine to reflect an anniversary, Christmas or another holiday. Could you celebrate a holiday or mark something positive in the world with your own twist on it? How about tweeting a photo of your employees in fancy dress celebrating winning a fun run for charity or baking a cake with a moustache on it to celebrate Movember (November's moustache-growing charity event)? Or you could show you are human by favouriting a joke from one of your followers, or posting your own joke of the day for your own followers to enjoy. Why not share some pictures of your employees as

one minute wonder SocialRank is a Twitter tool that lets you identify which of your followers interact with you most frequently. It analyzes replies and retweets as well as favourites, and it also lets you see whose are the most influential accounts. It will email you every month to let you know what is happening.

human beings? Perhaps post photos of the office party, that away day hiking along a trail path, the birthday cake someone baked in the office. Share the small moments as well as the big ones.

By the way, transparency is not the same as authenticity. You can be a real person and not share everything. We all have different relationships where we choose how much we share. Know your audience and let the relationship you want to build guide you as to what and how much you want to share.

Remember to monitor how effective these interactions are and what benefits accrue for your business.

Be fun, not just informative.

6.4

Hang out

Social media is supposed to be fun, so even if you are a stressed small-business owner, have fun. Become an enjoyable person to hang out with. The more you put in the more you'll get out of it.

■ Take part in the conversation. Answer questions and post some of your own. Let a conversation carry on and on until it develops a momentum.

■ Post at different times. Social media is not a nine-to-five job. Some people will read your posts at midnight and some in the middle of the day. If you are enjoying yourself it doesn't matter when you post.

■ Play with your hashtags on Twitter and make them entertaining. See if you attract new followers and make sure that if you say you are going to follow them back that you actually do so.

■ Respond to fans of your business. They will be pleased you have taken the time to respond and will become even more attached to your brand.

one minute wonder If you can't afford a graphic artist to make pretty pictures for your accounts, don't worry. You can use a specialist app to create images with editing tools that will allow you to crop and add text and look like a professional.

If you don't enjoy using social media, consider why. If you're boring yourself, the odds are you're boring others too. It's time to reassess what you're doing. Throw away the old content and start afresh. Start loving your customers and the conversations you have with them. Don't just become their friend. Make them your friends too!

Enjoy yourself and your fans and followers will soon pick up the energy.

6.5

Start a competition

Competitions get lots of people excited. They give you the chance to gain followers and expand your network while having fun.

■ Start with the end in mind. Be clear about what you want to get out of running a competition. Do you want to attract new followers or engage your existing ones?

■ What kind of promotion is right for your audience? How much effort will they want to put into it? Do you want them to work hard to win?

■ How much do you have to spend? A lot or a little? You can have a competition with a big prize at the end or a small promotion that perhaps runs for one day only.

case study Tom runs a small retail business. He decided to create a simple competition on Facebook where he asked his 'friends' to post jokes on his business page. The best joke of the week would win a voucher for one of his shops. He was amazed at the response he got. He doubled the number of his followers in a month as his friends forwarded the link to his

■ Make it easy to compete. If you want a wide audience, make the link to your competition bright, bold and easy to find and forward.
■ Have a clear deadline and stick to it. The rules of your competition should be clear to everyone.
■ Make it part of your brand. Not everyone will decide to take part but if they do visit your site to take a look, make sure that you have a clear message about your brand that they will remember.

You can create regular or one-off competitions. Perhaps you could create competitions with different levels of difficulty – from cryptic clues to simple sweepstakes to attract different types of participants. Make it as easy as possible to participate.

Create a daily or one-off competition.

page to their friends. It was such a simple idea but it got people talking about his business. He also noticed that traffic to his other sites increased as the visitors who just came for the jokes at first began to 'like' his photos and even post joke photos of their own, even though there was no prize on offer.

6.6

Be memorable

'Differentiation' is what makes you stand out in a crowded world. If you aren't different, no one is going to remember you and if you aren't memorable then you don't really have a brand.

So what if you don't have a million dollar budget? You can still make yourself prominent in the market. The little things are what matter. Do enough of them and the little things will make a big impression.

■ Create a strong profile. Pick a memorable screen name that represents your company. If you are going to personally represent your business make sure you use your real name and your own photo.
■ Get creative. Liven up your profile. Be funny. Be interesting. Be cute. Be exciting. Use great images, words and content.
■ Don't do it all by yourself. It is absolutely fine to engage a whole bunch of creative types.
■ Do something. Offer a free spa treatment to the first person to fill in your survey. Give away free meals to your local homeless hostel.
■ Host a breakfast Q and A with the CEO on Facebook. By giving your customers access to the top of your company, they'll feel their views count.

one minute wonder Tap into the celebrity or cultural buzz and rename your products for one day, one week or one month after famous people in history or in honour of a particular day. Tweet, blog and talk about what you are celebrating or commemorating.

■ Start Tweet Tuesday or Facebook Friday. On one day a week do something special for your customers on social media.
■ Why not suggest your fans name your new sandwich, sweet or ice cream for one day only? Suggest they post photos to match the name.

This is a chance to be original. Dare to be a little different!

Pay attention to the little things to create an impression.

6.7

Contribute to the conversation

In life you get back what you put in. You can't get on social media and expect to make an impact without effort. You have to be ready to put the work in and earn your followers. It is going to take a lot of work, so do what you enjoy. If you prefer tweeting to Facebook or Instagram, spend your time doing that. But if your other accounts are inactive for months it might be better to delete them.

■ **Respond to hashtags on Twitter.** Whether it is a hashtag you have started or someone else has started, why not respond? You can be serious or fun.

■ **Follow other people.** You don't have to follow everyone but do follow the influencers, innovators and community groups in your area. Your followers are very likely to look at who you are following for ideas.

■ **Use likes.** If someone posts a comment that you enjoy reading on your blog or Facebook page, then like it. They will appreciate your endorsement.

■ **Retweet.** If someone has mentioned you in a tweet and you like what they say, retweet it for your followers to see. But retweeting everything looks a little narcissistic.

one minute wonder Can you make your pictures go viral or trend? When something goes viral it means that people all over the net forward it to their friends without you asking them to. Videos, photos and ideas can all go viral. Something that is 'trending' is something popular on Twitter. Choose a fun hashtag (#) to create a campaign or post an image that people will want to send to friends.

■ **Don't down vote.** Clearly it would be self-sabotage to trash your followers' opinions. Like but don't dislike. If what has been posted is illegal then delete or block.

■ **Answer questions.** If someone has taken the time to ask, they want an answer. It is as rude not to answer an online message as it would be to ignore someone in person.

■ **Answer tweets.** They are as urgent as a ringing phone. Don't leave them hanging.

Build quality virtual relationships by investing some time and contributing to the conversation.

Follow web etiquette

Social media can seem a bit of a Wild West at first glance, with no rules and the freedom to be and say what you want. But there are rules and if you break them you'll get into trouble. Make sure you respect the community.

Don't bad-mouth your competitors, your customers or your own products and services. Pay attention to the law and above all be a decent, ethical business.

7.1

Be nice

This is probably the most important rule of social media. Because of the anonymity of much of social media you may be shocked by some of the comments you get on posts or by reactions to your tweets. But you don't need to bite back. Other people may choose not to be accountable for what they write or tweet but you can be. Take responsibility for everything that goes out under your name and if you make a mistake, hold your hands up.

■ **Don't troll.** A troll is someone who posts inflammatory, off-topic or rude comments to provoke conflict. Treat everyone as you would in real life and don't be a troll.

■ **Listen.** If someone has taken the time to post a comment that criticizes you or disagrees with you, take the time to listen and see if there is an issue that you can address.

■ **Don't sabotage.** Yes, people will notice your efforts to undermine your competitors and it will backfire.

■ **Don't feed trolls.** Even if your account is beset by trolls, don't feed the flames. If in doubt, don't post when you are feeling angry, drunk or exhausted.

"Don't say anything online that you wouldn't want plastered on a billboard with your face (or logo) on it" Erin Bury

one minute wonder Avoid the cheats. Some people buy Twitter followers or cheat the system to give themselves a thousand 'likes'. This makes them look popular for a while but everyone knows the game. Stay away from the cheats and don't cheat yourself. You won't gain anything at all.

Think before you act. What would my boss think about that Tweet? What would the executive team think about that blog? Will my competitors be pleased if I post that? How's that going to go down with my local community? Am I being respectful of all races and genders with that remark?

If it is too political, inflammatory or offensive, delete it before you post it.

Don't post when you are angry or exhausted.

7.2

Know your copyright

Most photographs and images such as diagrams, illustrations and graphics are protected by copyright. Text and music are similarly copyrighted. If it was created by someone else it does not belong to you. Copyright laws vary from country to country but generally you will need the permission of whoever owns the image before you can use it on the web.

Copyright is complicated. It may be owned by the person who created the image or their employer or publisher. Sometimes there are multiple copyright owners. Not everyone pays attention to copyright but as a business owner you need to. If you can't find the copyright holder copyright nevertheless still exists. If there is no copyright symbol this doesn't mean that copyright has expired.

The best rule to go by is: if you don't know who owns the copyright it isn't you. So don't post it. If you want to post it, you need to be licensed to do so, usually in return for payment. Basically, be careful. You can't go ahead and use, say, a picture of Harry Potter eating one of your ice creams or mash up music from *The Godfather* and put it on your company video.

one minute wonder If you want to make your social media campaign visual but can't afford to spend the time chasing copyright, why not engage a professional to make a short animation that shows how your product works. Even a few minutes will make an impression.

This may seem restrictive but there are images you can use and copyright only lasts for a certain number of years. In the UK, for example, images last for the life of the creator plus 70 years after their death. Remember, the law is on the side of the creator of the piece of work so it is much better that everything you post on social media is created by you.

If you don't know who owns it, don't post it.

7.3

Manage your crises

Sometimes things go wrong. It is not easy to manage a crisis in a business without the added responsibility of social media, but if you do run into a crisis you must be prepared to act quickly to contain it.

A small customer service issue which could be contained easily in a one-to-one chat can grow into a big crisis on social media platforms when a customer broadcasts their complaints to all their followers. A problem with a product can be talked about or mocked around the world on social media.

Deal with any issue quickly, honestly and put out the fire before your followers have time to fan the flames. Here are six steps to follow:

1 Think about what could go wrong in advance and assign responsibility for responding to customer service issues. Make sure whoever takes this role has appropriate training, including knowing about relevant regulations.

case study Greggs plc, a well-known bakery chain in the UK, provides a great example of how to use social media to turn a crisis to an advantage. One day in 2014, when someone replaced their logo with one from a parody site, it could have all gone wrong as the offensive phrase quickly went viral. But instead of panicking, Greggs posted a photo of doughnuts to their 88,000 followers

"Sometimes when you innovate, you make mistakes. It is best to admit them quickly, and get on with improving your other innovations" Steve Jobs

2 Risk Manage. Assess the level of the crisis. How severe is it? What impact could it have on your reputation and sales?

3 Respond quickly. As soon as you hear a complaint or learn about something going wrong, answer queries, put out a statement, show empathy, clarity and transparency. Listen, talk and follow up.

4 Monitor and measure the response. Check if what you have done so far has contained the issue. Show that you are willing to correct what has gone wrong.

5 When the crisis is over, don't sit back and think that's it. There may still have been damage to your reputation. Assess what needs to be done to rebuild and restore good customer relations and your good reputation.

6 Review what happened after the crisis is over. How can you learn and grow as a business?

Think about the plans you have in place to manage a crisis.

saying 'Hey @GoogleUK, fix it and they're yours. #FixGreggs.' Soon #FixGreggs trended and Google responded with a picture and the message 'Whoops! Sorry @GreggstheBakers. #FixGreggs #FixedGreggs #AteGreggs.' After the crisis was averted **PR Week's** headline was 'Greggs gives lesson in Twitter crisis management'.

7.4

Keep up with the news

It is important for every business to keep an eye on what is going on in the real world. What's happening locally? Nationally? Internationally? Keep an eye out for news on natural disasters, terrorist attacks, local tragedies or political controversies.

It doesn't look good if you are shouting out your business message online about how great your cakes are at a moment when the public are focused on an earthquake. Or if you are tweeting about your promotion when the country is solemnly commemorating a war or present or past catastrophic event.

Think about the pictures you are posting. Could any of them be perceived as politically partisan during an election? Or inappropriate at another time? You want to make sure you avoid any negative perceptions about your brand when there is a tragic event.

If you have decided to use a scheduling service or a third party to post content for you on social media sites, make sure you turn it off when you hear about a national catastrophe. Otherwise you and your brand could be tarred by the idea that you have been so insensitive to the feelings of the people who use your product or service. In the worst-case scenario you could provoke a consumer boycott or some other

one minute wonder When you first start out, why not write some practice blogs? Pick five top audience groups and five top messages you want to get across. Write some blogs but don't post them. Come back to them after a month and reread them. Do you still want to post them? If in doubt, don't.

kind of backlash against your business. It's worth reiterating, in the world of social media, where ideas can go viral in seconds, a bad impression about a brand can spread fast. Even if you tweet or blog and then delete it, remember that people may have taken a screenshot of your initial post and kept it. What's posted on the web is hard to hide. Avoid creating the problem in the first place.

Keep an eye on the news to avoid a crisis.

7.5

Stop the muggers

There has been a rise in social media 'muggings' in recent years. That is the industry term for accounts which get hacked into or accessed without permission. Millions of social media profiles have been hacked over the last few years.

Once someone has got hold of your password and username then your reputation can be ruined in seconds. Hackers can post rude comments, insult your brand or followers, post pornographic photographs or send messages from your account. If you use the same password for multiple business or personal accounts then you are also setting yourself up for identity theft fraud.

Suppose a hacker posts a rude message from your account; even if hacking is common, do you think you are going to persuade everyone it wasn't you? Probably not. Make sure you protect your password and keep aware of the latest scams or it could take a long time to recover your reputation.

one minute wonder Don't log into your business account on a public machine on public Wi-Fi in a library or an internet café. Make sure that if you do have to log into your social media account that you remember to log out and keep account of who in the company knows the key passwords.

The simplest precautions are the best. It is much harder to crack a password that is a combination of letters and numbers and symbols, capital and small letters. Change it regularly and don't post any information such as a key birthday or company foundation day that could lead someone to guess the password.

Protect your account and change your password regularly.

7.6

Do good

Being in business and doing good aren't mutually exclusive. You can build your business, or your business profile, and do good. In fact, you can build your business profile by doing good. You can raise money or simply use hashtags to highlight an issue on Twitter. You can also, of course, make videos, take pictures, write blogs and use social media to send them viral and get people talking about the cause you support.

Celebrities (or their PR people) are great at harnessing the power of social media for a good cause. As long as you don't get involved in every campaign indiscriminately, it's a great way to get noticed and to reinforce your brand.

Here are three basic rules to follow:

1 Think about what cause you want to support and why. How does it fit in with your brand? Is it better to support a local or national cause?

2 Choose campaigns that are worthy but not over-political. An over-identification with any particular political stance could taint your brand.

"Your television can't hear you. We can" MTV India

one minute wonder Consider which causes are closest to your heart. What is the result you want? Do you want people to donate money or simply spread the word about an issue? Is this going to be a one-off event or do you want doing good to be at the heart of your business?

3 While posting adverts on Facebook just irritates people, an advert that helps a good cause at the same time helps you, too.

You can also recommend apps and sites to your followers. Check out apps like SocialVibe where your followers can donate to a good cause based on filling out surveys. With the platform AdCause you can decide to donate money from advertising tweets to a cause. With Rec.fm, your followers are taken to recommended products and a percentage of what they spend is donated to charity. Endorse For A Cause is similar; you recommend a product and part of the profit is donated to charity.

Use the power of social media to support a good cause.

Jargon buster

Blog

A piece of writing, similar to an article in a magazine, posted on a social media channel or on a website. Can generally be commented on if the writer allows.

Brand

The main factors that differentiate your business from those of your competitors.

Channel

The term used to describe the different social media platforms.

Comment

An opportunity for interaction with the writer of a blog or a tweet, generally found at the bottom of the post.

Dashboard

A way of monitoring and measuring the interactions followers have with your blogs.

DM

A Direct Message is a private message you can send on Twitter to someone who follows you and whom you follow.

Favourite

You can press a link (a star in Twitter) to show that you like another person's tweet or blog post. This will save what you have favourited.

Feed

The news feed or information feed that is shown in real time to a person or account. It contains news and updates from other users they follow.

Follower

When you choose to click on the follow button on an account and receive their news and updates.

Friend

A friend is someone who links with you on Facebook.

Group

A place on a channel where people with common interests can come together and share content and links.

Handle

As indicated by the @ symbol followed by a name; the name of an account on Twitter.

Hashtag

A word or phrase preceded by the symbol. It is a way of searching or highlighting a conversation others can join in with, particularly on the Twitter platform.

IRL

In Real Life. Not to be confused with URL, which is a reference to an address on the internet.

Link

An address to another website or piece of content that can be posted to your network or be put permanently onto your main website.

List

A way to group your followers together on Twitter so that it is easy to find old tweets.

Micro-blogging

A piece of content that is limited to a certain number of words, as on Twitter.

Page

A showcase you can set up on a channel such as LinkedIn where you can give a description of the main features of your business.

Post

A piece of writing, a photo or other content you have uploaded to display for public or private viewing.

Profile

A short biography or description of your business you can put at the top of your account. Can be funny or serious.

Reach

The number of people your social media content is actually seen by.

SEO

Search Engine Optimization is a way of increasing your likelihood of being found by search engines on the internet.

Status

A section at the top of an account where you can add text, links or a video or photo that you can use to tell your followers or friends about where you are and what you are doing or thinking about.

Trending

When a hashtag becomes very popular across a wide network of people it is said to be trending.

Tweet

A piece of writing of 140 characters or less used on Twitter. Retweet is when you send someone else's tweet to your followers.

Viral

A post or topic that is shared by lots of users and often picked up by other media as well.

Vlog

A video blog commonly posted on a video-sharing site such as YouTube. A vlogger is the term for someone who makes the vlog.

Further reading

Boyes, Carolyn, *Career Management* (HarperCollins Business, 2010) ISBN 978-0-00073-244-9

Handley, Ann, *Everybody Writes: Your Go-To Guide for Creating Ridiculously Good Content* (John Wiley, 2014) ISBN 978-1-11890-555-5

Kawasaki, Guy and Fitzpatrick, Kate, *The Art of Social Media: Power Tips for Power Users* (Mcgraw-Hill, 2014) ISBN 978-0-24119-947-3

Kerpen, Dave, *Likeable Social Media?: How to Delight your Customers, Create an Irresistible Brand and be Generally Amazing on Facebook (and Other Social Networks)* (McGraw-Hill, 2011) ISBN 978-0-07176-234-2

Lee, Jennifer, *The Right-Brain Business Plan: A Creative, Visual Map for Success* (New World Library, 2013) ISBN 978-1-57731-944-3

Macarthy, Andrew, *500 Social Media Marketing Tips: Advice and Strategy for Business* (CreateSpace, 2013) ISBN 978-1-48201-409-2

Purkiss, John and Royston-Lee, David, *Brand You: Turn your Unique Talents into a Winning Formula* (Pearson, 2012) ISBN 978-0-27377-769-4

Schaefer, Mark, *Social Media Explained: Untangling the World's Most Misunderstood Business Trend* (Mark Schaefer, 2014) ISBN 978-0-61584-003-1

Schaefer, Mark W., *Return on Influence: The Revolutionary Power of Klout, Social Scoring and Influence Marketing* (McGraw-Hill Education, 2012) ISBN 978-0-07179-109-0

Schaefer, Mark W., *The Tao of Twitter: Changing your Life and Business 140 Characters at a Time*, 2nd edn (McGraw-Hill Education, 2014) ISBN 978-0-07184-115-3

Schaefer, Mark W. and Smith, Stanford, *Born to Blog: Building your Blog for Personal and Business Success One Post at a Time* (McGraw-Hill, 2013) ISBN 978-0-07181-116-3

Walter, Ekaterina and Jessica, Gioglio, *The Power of Visual Storytelling: How to Use Visuals, Videos and Social Media to Market Your Brand* (McGraw-Hill Education, 2015) ISBN 978-0-07182-400-2

Yohn, Denise Lee, *What Great Brands Do: The Seven Brand-Building Principles that Separate the Best from the Rest* (Jossey-Bass, 2014) ISBN 978-1-11861-125-8

Websites

Adage.com
Advertising agency and marketing industry news

Adweek.com
Emarketer.com
Market research on digital media and Internet marketing

Mashable.com
A useful site where you can keep up with trends in social media marketing

Techcrunch.com
Ted.com
Find interesting talks on subjects including futurology, business and the digital worlds